The Wa. , ...
God

Looking Again at Baptism and Its
Connectedness with the Hebrew Scriptures

The Watery Road to God

Table of Contents

How this Book Works

This book is intended to be used in personal or small group settings. Each chapter explores the relationship between baptism and the stories of the Old Testament in the hope of drawing each and every one of us in to a greater understanding of what this moment in the life of a believer really is.

At the end of each chapter, there is a section called "Wading into the Text". These sections have questions that can be used in a small group or personal setting. When needed, additional commentary is given to help explain the context of various passages.

May you, your small group and your church be blessed through this study of what should be one of the most beautiful moments in the life of every believer.

Introduction

You have always known, somewhere deep down, that there had to be more. You have encountered His beauty in the frozen waterfalls or in the blossoming flowers at the break of spring. You have felt His pain when you have somehow missed the mark, falling short of the greatness you instinctively know you are called to. "Where can I encounter Him," you wonder? And, so your journey begins. A journey towards the Maker and Sustainer of everything starts today.

You have heard that He isn't too far away. "Just down the road, on the other side of the hill," a friendly neighbor tells you. "When you get to the fork in the road, you have to go left. It is the only way in to the town where He lives."

Along the way, you meet many interesting folks, all stating quite matter-of-factly that they live in the town you are traveling to. They live with Him. However, your excitement is soon diminished. The citizens of this town can't seem to agree on what happens at the fork in the road. Many agree with the first person you talked to: left is the only way. Others state that, in fact, the little path to the left isn't needed at all. Once you arrive at the fork, you are actually already in town! "There is a path to the right that you could take, if you feel the desire to let the other towns-people know you have arrived," they tell you. "But, it is optional and very much not essential."

Hearing such contrary terms, you may find yourself wishing you hadn't made the journey at all. No one seems to agree on how to get there, or where "there" even is!

This is what has happened with Christian baptism. People have started their journey toward God and have welcomed the faithful followers they encounter along the way, but when it comes to baptism, there is confusion as to where it leads, if it leads anywhere, and what the point of it is, if there is one.

There are many who say that baptism is simply the road on the left. It is a requirement, or a step in a process. It is a very simple step in a five-part process towards God. Do it, or you simply will never arrive to the place where God lives.

There are others who say that it isn't a needed path at all, like the path on the right. Do it if you like, just to keep with tradition, but there isn't really any depth or meaning to it. It is just a nice thing to do if one chooses, letting others know what God has already done in your life. Or, it is done to place membership at a local congregation. It has nothing to do with your relationship with God.

In this book, I want to suggest that there is a third path, or way, to understand baptism. One that Biblically blends both paths

9

to create a third one. Or, better put, a way of understanding that the two paths are actually part of a much larger road, the watery road to God. This isn't a road to nowhere special, nor is it simply a required path with no scenery or beauty. Instead, the watery road is one of the most powerful, precious and, ultimately, desirable experiences of our walk with God. It is neither mundane but necessary, nor superfluous and optional.

Baptism, as described in the Bible, invites the seeker to come and walk along its path, look and see where the road leads, and soak in the beauty that God has put on exhibit all around it. It is not just a path we need to take. It is a path we long to take; our hearts cry out to us to keep walking into the waters, to go deeper until we are completely covered in its life-changing power. There, in the depths, we feel its weight wash over us with cleansing waves of love, penetrating our very souls and purifying us from all our wrongs. It is deeply profound, wondrously beautiful and as needed as water, food, shelter and love.

For too long, the church hasn't been looking at the path in its entirety. We have been focusing on one part, causing some to conclude that the path is useless and others to determine that the path is not powerful or beautiful; it is simply a functional step, full of man-made traditions and void of beauty.

It is my hope to show that baptism has been part of God's plan from the beginning. We will take a look at the Old Testament and see how these waters show God's justice and mercy; how they show His judgement and cleansing. Together, we will capture the beauty, power and place of baptism for every believer.

11

rob coyle

Chapter 1

Baptize the Earth, Baptize Me

In the heavens, a storm was mounting. The once blue sky with the bright, brilliant sun was starting to grow grey and dark. Earth's closest star now hides itself behind the billowing clouds, brimming with an ominous darkness. For the first time, the heavens looked frightening, seeming to threaten from afar.

The sun may be hiding, but the people in the valleys and in the hills, where the clouds began to accumulate, had no place to run. Though safety was sought after, it was nowhere to be found. Everywhere they turned, darkness filled the sky.

Before the torment had begun to build in the heavens, the dark clouds of wickedness had billowed in the hearts of men: a storm that had been brewing for quite some time. They grew larger and larger, filling their minds and souls with the blackness of selfishness and violence. Brutality and wickedness was the guiding rule of the day. Oppression and greed, slavery and malice continually fueled the motives behind every action and thought of man. But, God had a plan. It seemed brutal and unloving, but His plan remained steadfast. Destruction and devastation were looming in the sky. The crust of the earth was about to be opened, awakening the powerful and strong instruments of God's justice. God was about to shake the whole world with His wrath. The violence and evil of man had reached full capacity. Something needed to be done.

There, in the midst of such wickedness and cruelty, lived a family of eight. Though the darkness of sin and oppression surrounded them at every turn, they had not relinquished their desire to do good. The father of the nomadic family, Noah, had chosen a different path to walk than the other roads around him. Noah walked with God.

"The end of all flesh has come before me," God told Noah sorrowfully. "Men have filled the earth with violence, now I will destroy them with the earth." God instructed Noah on what to do. He was to build an ark, fill it with animals and survive the judgment that was soon to come.

Then it began. What was at first a single drop of rain turned into a downpour. The sound of thunder filled the skies. Lightning struck the ground, filling the people with fear and horror. The villagers and town dwellers began to scurry about in all directions in hopes of finding a shelter from the wrath of God, but every hiding place was soon penetrated and flooded with water. The earth started to shake and tremble. Large aquifers of water, hidden under the earth, were opened and giant fountains shot up into the obscure and clouded sky. The land was continually covered more and more with water, ever chasing them to higher ground. There wasn't any safe place to hide; there was nowhere to run. The waters of

17

justice had broken in to every part of the land. Eventually, the waves crashed upon the final human heart. And there in the waters, the wickedness that had made this person's heart its home died. The sin of earth had been dealt with. It drowned in the ubiquitous water. The good creation of God had been cleansed.

Noah and his family, though, were safe. Though the waves crashed against the boat, rocking it back and forth, they were unharmed. Life in the future would be different. It would be better. Humanity would know that God will deal with mankind's wickedness. God will not tolerate evil and violence forever. He will judge. The sin of man will be dealt with.

What must it have been like to be on that boat? The door is closed and the window shut, but in the darkness you can hear the sounds of God's judgment literally being poured out. Days and days go by, but the rain is relentless. It just keeps coming down, covering, immersing and destroying everything it touches. Then, as quickly as it came, it stops. By the time you get off the boat, new life has already started to grow. No more violence fills the land. No more wickedness of man threatens. The earth has been renewed and the great creation project has started afresh.

The apostle Peter tells us that we don't have to try and imagine what it might have been like to be in the flood. In baptism, he says, we experience the same washing. Covered in water, God purges us of all our sin.

We see him make this point in his first letter to "the pilgrims of the Dispersion." In 1 Peter chapter 3, verses 20-21, we read that eight souls, Noah and his family, were saved through (or by) water. The flood of Noah was a signpost, pointing to the reality to come. It may be hard to accept, but our baptism is the true flood. One day, a day God had in mind all along, He was going to send His waters to cover

19

us, to cleanse and purge us of all our sin and wickedness. He was going to wash us with clean water to refresh us and give us life.

It wasn't the ark that saved Noah and his family. If he had built the ark, but there had been no flood, the earth would still have been polluted by the sin of man. There might have been a massive and wonderful boat, but it would have served no purpose. No, it was the water that did the work. It was the water that sought out every hiding place and judged the sin of humanity. The ark allowed Noah and his family to experience the other side of justice: mercy.

Baptism is our opportunity to experience the flood. We look deep within ourselves and recognize the need to be washed clean. This isn't a ceremonial washing, cleansing just the body. Nor is it a work whereby we can boast of how great we are. No, it is deeper and more wonderful. It is the moment when we ask God to wash over us with His holiness and love. We ask Him to penetrate every hidden place in our lives, places where sin might be hiding, hoping to escape His wrath. In effect, we ask God to drown and condemn our sinfulness in His judgment, but to revive us with His mercy.

Peter says that this is what happens. God condemns the sin within, but, through the resurrection of Jesus, we can be raised to life[1], clean and ready to live God's creation project.

If you have already entered the dangerous and loving waters of God, this should be a moment of constant strength, a time you can look to and remember that your life is no longer the same. Everything is different now. Everything is new. Just as God had called Noah to go and fill the earth, you are also called to go and fill the earth with God's loving reign.

---

[1] 1 Peter 1:3-5

For those who haven't yet stepped out into the deep: God is waiting. His justice and mercy are waiting. Listen to the sound of the crashing waves of God's cleansing power. Hear the thunderous noise and know that God longs to overwhelm you with His holiness and wash you clean. He intends to and will condemn every sin you carry. And He will wash over you with His grace. You will be safe. By His son, Jesus the Christ, you are engulfed not only in the judgment of sin, but in the mercy of His cleansing love and mercy.

Baptism isn't merely a step, part of a formula or program found just to the left of the path. Nor is it an optional trail, just to the right, powerless and useless. The baptism road is broader and greater, filled with power, purpose and glorious beauty. Just as God baptized the earth, we invite Him to also baptize us. Wash over us and give us new life. Cleanse us from our sinful past and give us hope for our future.

The watery road to God is immensely meaningful and together we cry out to Him: "Just as You baptized the earth; baptize me."

Wading into the Text: The Epistles of Peter

Stories often impact us and form us in ways that we do not anticipate. For Peter, it seems that no story from his Jewish history was more impactful than that of the flood. In his two short letters, he makes mention of this moment three different times: once in his first letter and twice in his second.

Peter is writing to both Jewish and Gentile followers of the Christ who were undergoing suffering and persecution as they struggled to live the holy life to which they were called. As they look around and contemplate their lives, it may have been tempting to go back to their old way of life. Surrounded by sin and oppression, it may have seemed as though God would never judge and redeem: that He would never make things right. They could feel their hopes slipping away, slowly giving way to the desire to turn back. Peter tells them not lose hope. He tells them to consider the flood.

Read 2nd Peter 2:4-11

In what ways might a persecuted follower of Christ be encouraged by these passages?

How does the flood of Noah encourage us today to continue living the life God has called us to? How does it encourage us to hold on to hope?

Read 2nd Peter 3:1-13

Have you ever felt like the wickedness of man has been going unpunished? How might meditating on Noah and the flood help you to see that your perception of life is incorrect, or is at best short sighted?

It is often easy to look around and see the evil of others. Have you ever looked at your own life and wished that something could be done about your own sin?

God purified the earth with water in the days of Noah. What is God's plan to purify the earth more wholly and completely according to verse 10?

According to verse 13, what is the hope that we are all called to look forward to and eagerly await?

Read 1 Peter 3:18-21

Contrary to what many may intuitively think, Noah and his family were not saved by the ark. It is thought that the ark saved them from the water, but Peter says that it is actually the water that saved them.

In what way did the water save Noah and his family?

27

When considering this passage along with the ones read in 2nd Peter, how might the flood have cleansed the earth, and in what way does it now cleanse us?

How might knowing that our baptism was the actual flood God imagined all along help you to better live for Him?

Chapter 2

The True Exodus

A long, hard day had passed. It was like so many other days that had gone before. Now, around a small table as the sun is setting, a meal and stories are shared. All the family has gathered around to eat the evening meal and listen as grandfather tells stories of long ago.[2] Everyone sits in silence and, as though dreaming, hears his words as he harkens to times past: times when life was different; times when life was better.

There, with calloused hands and sore backs, the family listens to their elder tell them of one of the greatest times of their history. He speaks to them of Abraham, Isaac and Jacob. They heard about how God had led them and saved them from all trouble. They heard of how Abraham too was once in Egypt and how he left more blessed than he had arrived. They heard about Joseph who was once a servant and a

---

[2] Before the Old Testament was written down, stories were told to pass on information.

prisoner, but later became one of the greatest leaders Egypt had ever known. Joseph saved the people from certain death as the seven-year famine destroyed all hopes of life. Egypt was a land of provision and protection. All who came to this land found life.

The stories sounded so foreign to the younger generation. Nearly half a millennium had passed since Joseph saved the nations and so much had changed for the Israelites who had decided to stay in Egypt. With Joseph dead and new Pharaohs running the empire, the Hebrew nation found themselves at the mercy, or lack thereof, of cruel and oppressive leaders. The land that once offered hope for the future now held only the promise of slavery and dehumanizing labor.

As the evening stories would end, the family would sit and wonder if God would ever come back to them. Would they ever experience the blessing of Abraham in this land of cruelty? Would they ever be like Joseph: once a slave but later free and reigning? God had led their ancestors, but it seemed that He had forgotten about them. Would salvation ever come?

As the work grew harder and the Pharaoh ever more evil, the firstborn child of God, Israel, cried out to Him, the maker of heaven and earth. They had to have wondered if their voice ever made it to His ears. Had God heard their cry for mercy, relief and comfort? Had He heard their desperate cry for freedom and justice, or had their heart's cry dissipated into the night sky?

The Pharaoh and leader of Egypt had grown paranoid and fearful over the years. As the Jews multiplied in number, he saw no choice but to command the newborn boys be killed, drowned in the River Nile. But, there in the water floated their deliverer. The answer to their prayer was only months old, floating in a basket, hidden in the reeds on the bank of the river. His name was Moses, for had been drawn out of the water. Their hope for salvation was found in the water.

As Moses grew older, his love for his brethren grew as well. Though he had lived most of his life as an Egyptian leader, adopted by Pharaoh's daughter, he spent his early years with the Jews, his family. He loved them. One day, he was sickened by the treatment of his flesh and blood. In anger, he struck and killed an Egyptian. Word of his attack spread. The news made its way to Pharaoh and Moses went on the run. It was all part of God's plan. God had heard their cries and was mounting a rescue.

Moses had found a new land, a wife and peace. He started a family and may have believed that his time in Egypt was nothing but a life lived long ago: just a fading memory. But, he would be wrong. Tucked away in the mountains, the angel of the Lord awaited him. The great "I AM" had spoken. The redemption of Israel was at hand. Moses had been chosen to bring God's children home and he started his journey back to the land of slavery.

No one was prepared for what was about to take place. The wrath of God was about to be put on display and the freedom of the Hebrews was about to be realized.

There on the banks of the Nile, the same river that had swallowed the innocent baby boys and delivered him as an infant, Moses met Pharaoh. Moses strikes the waters with his staff. The river turns red, flowing with blood. The fish die and the stench of death blankets the land of slavery.

But the Great "I AM" is not done; He is just getting started. He sends frogs, lice, flies, pestilence, boils, hail and locusts. With every plague, Pharaoh's resolve is more hardened. The Hebrews belonged to him. He would not let them go. The child drawn from water would not save them.

The 9th plague is upon them. Darkness falls upon the land of the Egyptians. It is impenetrable, thick, tangible and stronger than the sun. The citizens of that country sit as though frozen in place, unable to move. The darkness of Pharaoh's heart still has not found its equal. He will not let them go.

Then it happens. God's destroyer is unleashed in the town. At midnight, he goes about, meticulously entering the homes of the Egyptians and kills every firstborn child and animal in the land. However, the Israelites are safely sealed from this fate. The blood of the lamb was on their doorposts and lentels. The destroyer sees the blood and passes over.

The weeping heard that night was great. Not a single home was left untouched. Everyone had suffered loss. Pharaoh had finally met his match and was at long last ready to let them go. This change of heart would not last long. He would soon change his mind.

The newly freed Jews had made it as far as the waters of the Red Sea when they heard the sound of chariots and horses charging from behind. They looked and saw the armies of their former oppressor heading straight for them. They were trapped. An impassable sea lies in front of them. Just behind them approaches an army bent on slaughter and enslavement. Overcome with fear and anger, the former slaves lash out at Moses. The dangerous thoughts of doubt are swirling in their minds. "We could have died just as easily in Egypt," they would cry out. The water seems to have doomed them to destruction.

Here, at the Red Sea, the God of Abraham, Isaac and Jacob would perform one final act of judgment against the Egyptians. The man who had been drawn out of water would now lead them *through* the water. The stories

37

of old would now become their stories. The God who once led their ancestors would now lead them. He would bring them from slavery to freedom. He would exodus them from the land of bondage to the land of beauty. Their Egyptian oppressors would never be seen again.

The angel that had led them out of Egypt and to the sea now moved to their back. It formed a massive, unpassable cloud that issued darkness on the one side, but light on the other. It was like an enormous pillar made of cloud and fire. The children of God were safe as the pillar blocked the way and kept the enemy at bay.

As Moses reached out his hand, a wind began to blow. The east wind blew stronger and stronger, pushing against the Red Sea that had them trapped and cornered. The water was pushed back so strongly that it divided the waters of the sea and dried the once wet land below. As night fell, the Jews began to cross over, leaving the land of slavery. With water all around them and covered with the cloud of God, they made their way to freedom.

Pharaoh made one last attempt to hold on to his power. With the new day dawning, they see that the protective cloud of the Lord was no longer blocking the way. This would be the last morning any of them mount their chariots. The very waters that had brought salvation to the Jews now provided destruction to the oppressor. Moses reaches out his hands one last time. The waters come crashing down on the enemies of God and the enslaver of His children. In confusion and haste, they are crushed under the weight of the water. God's children are safe at long last; they are free. Their cries had been heard and their salvation delivered. The water had saved them; their longings for God to act as He had in the lives of their ancestors had come true. The stories they heard from the elders in their families had become their stories.

The watery road to God is wider than we have expected. Often, it is more powerful than we have ever known. Paul tells us in 1 Corinthians 10:1-2, that the saved children of God were baptized that day into Moses. They were covered in cloud and surrounded by water. There was no other way across from slavery to freedom. The waters billowed up in mercy for the Jews and came rushing down in justice on the nation of slavery.

He goes on in chapter 12, verse 13 to tell us that we are all baptized into one body, that of Jesus the Christ. We are a new exodus people. Our former lives, before our exodus, were filled with long hard days of living in a way that is less than human. Our acts and thoughts were sinful, filled with the constant knowledge that we have missed the mark. Like them, we needed someone to come and take us through the water to the other side. We needed to be set free.

The great biblical scholar of our day, NT Wright, points out that, in fact, the very beginning chapters of Romans are actually a subtle reenactment of the exodus of Israel.[3] Romans starts by showing that all people actually find themselves in the miserable land of slavery. Sin has infected our lives and we have become its slave. In chapter 6, we find ourselves on the shore of the Red Sea. Certain death, the wage of sin, pursues us from behind and the only way out is through the frightening and strange waters in front of us. Here, we enter the waters of baptism. Here, in the water, God performs His mighty work in our lives. The part of our heart that has lived for sin and self now finds itself struggling for air. But it is not able to breathe. Like a reflex, it twitches

---

[3] The New Inheritance According to Paul, Bible Review 14.3, June 1988

and inhales the judgment of God. The sinful man has died in the water. Our Egyptian heart no longer beats or threatens to drag us back to the old land. It is dead.

Jesus has died for our sins and we share in His death when we are buried in the water with Him. He meets us there and brings us out of the water. He brings us to a new life: a life filled with His Spirit and able to live the way God has always intended us to live. We can finally be free from sin so we can serve our God. In Christ, there is no condemnation. Death has been defeated and new life has been gifted.[4]

One could argue that there is no way to the land of freedom without going through the water. And, of course, they would be right for making such an argument. Truly, there is no argument to be had. But, that would be focusing on a small part of the road, just to the

---

[4] Romans 6-8

left of where we stand. It is part of the road,
but it is not the whole road.

When you are sitting on the shores of
the Red Sea and recognize the reality and
gravity of your situation, you long to cross over
to the other side. You hear the footsteps of
death marching toward you and you want to
jump in the water and let God do His work. You
are not contemplating whether or not you need
to. You see the broader road and wish to
experience the power of God.

Jesus is in the water, ready to guide us
through to freedom. At His call, we dive in and
experience Him. With the water rushing all
around us, we get what our sin has deserved all
along. The punishment of sin is death, and in
the watery sea, we die. It may seem morbid or
even grotesque, but the sinful man's heart
stops beating in the water. His lungs stop
breathing. He is no longer alive. Instead, God

makes us again; He recreates us. We get to start over and live the resurrection life.

Baptism beckons us to come. It calls us to wade into the waters and let justice and mercy wash over us. In justice, it removes the sin that has so deeply imbedded itself in our lives. In mercy, it fills us with new life and we can rejoice in knowing that in Christ, there is no condemnation. We have been released from the land of bondage and set free.

This isn't just a required religious work or ritual. And it is so much more than some optional act that one can chose to do if so inclined. On the contrary, baptism is a work that God does. It frees us so that we can serve Him. It is beautiful and powerful. It should be the desire of our heart to plunge in and watch God justly and mercifully act in our lives. The true exodus has come.

Wading into the Text

1 Corinthians is a wonderful book written to a struggling group of believers who are on the verge of losing all identity with the message of Christ. Though still referred to as "saints", it seems that their actions and lifestyles were far from holy. Like the Hebrews of old, many had desired to turn back and return to the common and, oddly, comforting land of slavery. Paul tells these followers to consider the Exodus.

Read 1 Corinthians 10:1-13

In what way was all of Israel baptized?

What does it mean to be baptized into Moses?

According to this passage, how can we know that the exodus from Egypt was not complete?

The baptism into Moses freed them from the land of slavery, but it did not free them to live as God's people. According to chapter 12:1-13, the Christian is baptized into one body, that of the Messiah Jesus. How is this exodus different and better than that of Moses?

Read Romans 6:1-7

What does Paul say happens to us when we are immersed in the water?

The Egyptian slaves were buried in the water and never returned. In what way are we also buried?

What does it mean to be buried with the Messiah; to be crucified with Him?

How does the resurrection of Jesus make our Exodus more complete?

What part of your life, or perhaps even the life of the church, needs to be reckoned as dead so you and the church can live for God?

Chapter 3

The True Flesh Removal

ad to God

"Look now towards the heavens and count the stars if you can. So shall your descendants be."[5]

The promise seemed to be undoable. He was already quite old when he heard the news and passed the night in a deep, dark sleep. Now, years later, too much time had passed and the hope of a son seemed to have vanished into the horizon just like his homeland had when he journeyed from the place of his family. Now, old age had caught up with him and his wife, convincing them both that they would never see the promise fulfilled. There in their dwellings they sat, far from home, wondering what the future might bring. The dream of a child of their own, a child of promise, was surely dead. In desperation, they made plans to fulfill the promise of God by another means. The uncertainties of tomorrow overwhelmed their minds.

[5] Genesis 15:5

It was a decision they lived to regret. Abraham and Sarah, as they would soon be known, initiated a plan to finish what God had started over a decade before. Their servant, Hagar, would bear them a son. They came together and a son, Ishmael was given. However, he was not the son of promise.

God's covenant with Abraham for all humanity would not be fulfilled through the sin of fear and doubt. It was to be fulfilled through faith, courage and patience. Indeed, it would come so that all the world would know that God, the maker of heaven and earth, had done this. No will or plan of man would do. Only the power and will of God could accomplish such an impossible task.

The covenant was nothing short of spectacular: through Abraham, now 100 years of age, all the nations of the earth would be blessed. A world that had been overrun with sin and failure since the time of Adam would somehow find it's restoration in and through his family.

As a sign to Abraham, the God over all of creation introduced a strange procedure. Part of the flesh of man needed to be removed. The mysterious connection between sin and flesh had been established. When a person removes the flesh, they are walking in faith, recognizing that only God is able to do the needed work. They are stating that Isaac will come and with him the blessings of God. The practice of circumcision had been instituted, even before the law of Moses had been given.

Throughout the years, this practice was observed. It was to be a constant sign that one day, sin would be dealt with. One day, the human heart would be cleansed of sin and flesh would finally be able to serve God whole-heartedly. As were most practices, circumcision was only a sign of things to come.

For the children of Israel, circumcision would come to represent less than it was intended to mean. Instead of a sign of a future hope promised by God Himself, it had become a badge and mark that you were part of God's family. It had become a rite of passage, a law that marked you out as the chosen, elect people of God. Those without the mark were without God: outside the family, having no part in the blessed fellowship with the Father.

But circumcision was so much more than this. It was the promise that one day, God would deal with sinful flesh completely and fully. God would perform this same ritual on the hearts of men, removing the flesh that is enslaved to sin. The Surgeon would carefully and precisely remove the sinful flesh that has surrounded and enclosed the heart, exposing it to the life-giving love of the Father.

There, in old age and no other option other than to trust God, Abraham removes the flesh from his body. Abraham has faith in the faithfulness of a God who can do anything; even bring life where there isn't any to be seen. With nothing but faith expressed in a sign, the promised son does come. Isaac is born.

God's prophet, Jeremiah, makes it clear that circumcision was never just a "ritualistic procedure" that He desired.[6] Ultimately, God wants a heart that belongs to Him.[7] He wants a child who loves Him with all the force and might he has. All who fall short of this love for God (and all have fallen short) have failed to achieve a true circumcision. The skin is removed, but the sin remains. The sinful flesh is still holding the heart captive. And as we have seen previously, sin must be punished.

So it is that we often find ourselves feeling exactly and precisely as Paul had described in Romans 7. The weight of our sinful

---

[6] Jeremiah 9:25-26
[7] Deuteronomy 10:12-16

flesh is more than we can bear; it seems impossible to escape from. We see the good to be done, yet find ourselves somehow incapable of doing it. Yet, we see the bad that we know we shouldn't do and our sinful flesh seems to always find a way to do it. With Paul, we cry out, "Oh wretched man that I am! Who will deliver me from this body of death?" In other words, when will God do what He said He would do from the beginning? When would the sign of circumcision find its fulfillment just as the flood and exodus had? When will we be saved?

Praise be to God; our salvation is found in Christ! In Christ Jesus our Lord, God has performed the needed surgery and removed the sinful flesh that has held our hearts captive. Just as one might go under before an operation, we find ourselves going under the clean, purifying water of baptism. There in the water, the true removal of flesh is found. Christ, the seed of Abraham, Son of God, is there to fulfill the promise made long ago. A true circumcision is performed. The sinful flesh of your heart is cut away. You are finally free to live. You are forgiven and made new. Just as Christ died in the flesh, so do you as you are buried with Him in those wondrous waters. Just as Christ rose from the dead, so do you. The promise to Abraham and the sign of circumcision have been fulfilled.

In him also you were circumcised with a circumcision made without hands, by putting off the body of the flesh, by the circumcision of Christ, [12] having been buried with him in baptism, in which you were also raised with him through faith in the powerful working of God, who raised him from the dead. [13] And you, who were dead in your trespasses and the uncircumcision of your flesh, God made alive together with him, having forgiven us all our trespasses, [14] by canceling the record of debt that stood against us with its legal demands. This he set aside, nailing it to the cross.[8]

We find ourselves once again at the fork in the road. It now looks just a little wider

---

[8] Colossians 2:11-14 ESV

than it had before. The roads to the left and the right are barely able to be seen: the beauty and power of the watery road to God has seamlessly made them part of the whole. We are finally starting to see that there is truly only one path, and it is magnificent. We can see where the path is leading, and the town looks more wonderful than we have imagined. Our hearts can truly belong to Him. We hear the words ripple upon the waters. They invite us to come all the way in, until we are completely under. There in the water, Christ meets us; frees us. He opens us up and removes the sinful flesh that has for too long reigned in our hearts.

The battle is over and the condemnation is gone. Just when it seemed as though all hope was lost, God did the impossible. He made a heart so obviously wrong, right. He made a flesh that could love. He made a flesh that could be free. Our flesh has been set free from death. We are finally alive.   We have finally received the true circumcision.

Wading Into the Text

Read Jeremiah 9:25-26

Jeremiah prophesied about the impending judgement of God upon His chosen people by Babylon. Why is it that both the circumcised and uncircumcised will be punished? What is the circumcision that is needed, and what does this mean?

Read Deuteronomy 30:6

How does this verse from the Law of Moses help us in understanding what the sign of circumcision was meant to signify? What has

61

God truly wanted from His children from the very beginning?

Read Romans 2:28-29 (and greater context as needed)

How does one become a "Jew" inwardly? What does this mean, and how might this realization help us to remember that our boast is in God, not in ourselves?

Read Colossians 2:11-14

When does Christ, the Messiah, perform the true circumcision in the heart of the believer?

While many might claim that baptism is a work, like the law, Paul says that in baptism, we receive the true circumcision prophesied centuries before, and longed for since the practice was made law. In what way is baptism a sign that the law has been fulfilled?

How does knowing that we have been given the circumcision of Christ help us to better live our life more fully for God?

Chapter 4

New Clothes

The air is bursting with anticipation. Life is filled with an eager expectation that God will finally do what the prophets from half a millennium before had spoken about. There in captivity, behind 90-foot-high walls, you wait to see what God will do. You long to see the God that freed your family from the oppression of slavery in Egypt to act again on your behalf. You know that you belong to the freed people, but Babylon seems to have proven that you are no longer that people destined to live free; that God is no longer the God who saves, redeems and restores.

In depression, you hear the oppressor talk about how many of your family and countrymen, just a generation before you, died in the second siege of Nebuchadnezzar. Sick from epidemics and starving from a lack of provision, nearly a million lost their lives before the city was ever invaded. As soon as they were too weak and disease-ridden to put up a fight, the king of Babylon, Nebuchadnezzar, overtook the city. He destroyed the walls with fire and left the temple in rubble. It was then that the rest of your family was taken captive and brought to the land of bondage and brutality. There you were given the rags of oppression with which to clothe yourself.

For almost 70 years, your people have lived as slaves in a strange land. For nearly 70 years, you and your brethren have worn the attire of the afflicted. The garments of God were exchanged, by force, for the garments of bondage. For those who are willing and able, you see those robes as the clothing of sin itself: a constant reminder that your life is far from what it should be.

Before the fall of your city and country, your family had abandoned their one true God. They worshipped false gods on the hills that surrounded the once great city of Jerusalem. They forsook Him, and it seems as though He has done the same. The prophets spoke about seeing God Himself withdraw from the temple in fiery wheels. With your city destroyed and the temple of the living God lying in ruins, the prophecies must have been true. Truly, He, the great King, must be gone.

You look at yourself and wish your life were different. Your clothing is a constant reminder that you are nothing but a sinner in an alien land. You long for the time when your clothing can be that of a free people. You long to go back to the land of your forefathers, rebuild the house of God, and serve Him.

Then, one night, your mind is filled with dreams and visions stranger than any you have ever had before. You see a great host of horses walking through a hollow filled with myrtle trees. They roam all the earth, and have found that it is seemingly at peace. But you wonder how it is that the world can be at peace when the people of God are scattered and held against their will. In your dream, God declares that He is about to act justly on your behalf.

You see another vision of four horns and craftsmen. You are told by an angel that these horns are the empires that have held the Hebrew nation captive, but they will be driven out in fear by the craftsmen. There is hope stirring up in your heart, but your filthy rags remind you that the great dreams are not yet able to be realized in your life. Perhaps in your darker moments, your filthy rags try to convince you that the dreams you have are nothing but that: visions and hopes. The reality is you are nothing but a slave without a home to go back to.

You hear the call of God in your dreams, calling you and your countrymen to arise and depart the land of the north, the land of the captors. Flee from them. God is going ahead of you and will dwell with you in the land of your fathers, the wonderful land of promise. He

71

Himself will be a wall around you, like a wall of fire. He will surround you with His glory, greater than the glory of the temple that was there before in the days of Solomon.

Your name is Zechariah and God Almighty has been speaking to you through the night. He has been aroused from His holy mountain and is about to sweep through the land with His freeing power. The time is coming when you will change your clothes.

Amongst the many visions you have had, there is one that is seems to stand out. You are shown the high priest, a man named Joshua, standing before the Angel of the Lord. Joshua is wearing the garments of slavery, rebellion and sin. They are dirty, covered in smoke and soot, as though pulled from a fire. Beside him, just to his right, stands Satan, the great accuser. He is there to oppose Joshua: to accuse him before the Lord as a man unholy and fully unworthy. The sinister force of malice that has fueled the evil empires of man now stands ready to try and thwart Israel's hopes for a better, freer future.

The accuser stands there in the midst and looks to have an unbeatable case. Joshua, Israel's representative before God, is indeed filthy and undeserving of God's freeing power. Like the prophet Isaiah stated, his righteous acts are like filthy rags.[9] His sin and shame are as obvious as the dirt on his robes that declare him to be a son of bondage. Then God makes an unexpected move.

"Rid Joshua of the filthy garments of slavery," He says. "Put royal, clean and holy garments on him and wrap his head with a clean turban. See, I have removed your sin and iniquity."[10]

The words from Almighty God were as shocking as they were needed. Pure grace had

---

[9] Isaiah 64:6
[10] Zechariah 3

been poured out. Clean and priestly clothes had been given. Like a prodigal son come home, the Father has forgiven the sins of the past. He has given the clothing of a son.

Now, with new garments, Joshua is able to serve God without accusation. There is now no condemnation Satan can bring against him that will stand. God has overcome. His people are free to return and live in His presence. They are covered in His grace, clothed in His holy garments of hope and peace.

Paul tells us in Colossians 3 that after God has removed the sinful flesh from our bodies in baptism, with the true circumcision, we are now alive in Christ. If we are alive in Christ, and if our lives are truly hidden with Christ in God, then we are to rid ourselves of the garments and robes of our old life, just as Zechariah had seen happen to Joshua in his vision from heaven. Paul warns us not to be taken captive by our former way of life, like those in the Babylonian exile, but rather to exchange our stained and dirty clothes for new clothes that are fitting for those who are renewed in knowledge according to the image of Him who created us anew.

Paul says that in Christ, through baptism, we are now alive with the Messiah. We are part of a new family where all the former ways of life are now different. We are part of a new man that has removed the clothing of anger, hate, evil and blasphemy. The old rags of our past were once stained with idolatry, lies, fornication, unholiness, wicked desires and envy. The new robes of God are as soft as tender-mercy, kindness, humility and patience. They are gentle to the touch, like forgiveness and love.

Before God, we stood like so many who had gone before us. The clothing of our old lives was filthy before Him. But now, we have been able to rid ourselves of the attire of sin, exile and death. We can now put on life: a life that is only found in Christ. We are clean. Our clothes are new.

Standing at the watery road to God, it is now difficult to see any diversion in the path at all. You begin to wonder why all the kind folk along the journey seemed to have seen a fork in the road, right in the place you now stand. Having peered deeply down the trail, it is now much more expansive and wondrous than you yourself had ever known. All the descriptions you heard before fail to describe its beauty and power. They not only fail, they didn't even try.

As before, the waters beckon you to come: come and be a part of a new man, a new family that is adorned with new robes that are fresh and clean. Robes that are designed to live the life God has re-created you to be. Will you go? Will you plunge yourself into His waters of mercy and justice and let Him give you the clothes of freedom and love?

Wading into the Text

Read Colossians 3:8-14 (and greater context as needed)

Have you ever been so dirty that you absolutely needed a completely new set of clothing?

Have you ever helped someone in need get new, clean clothes?

Paul tells us in Colossians that in baptism, our old life is dead and buried. We now live a new life, a forgiven life, a resurrected life.

What are the old garments that we are to remove, or "put off", now that we are alive with Christ?

77

What are the new clothes that we are to put on?

How does the imagery of new clothes help you as you either look forward to your baptism, or look back on it?

Chapter 5

The New, True Creation

It was as perfect a place as could be found anywhere. The land was filled with life, spoken into existence by the God of the universe, maker and keeper of all things. Before time, space or matter existed, God was there. In the nothingness, He spoke words of power and precision. At His utterance, the "nothingness" produced "thingness". The beginning had begun. Creation was springing up inexplicably.[11] The abundant life Jesus spoke of was growing all around.[12]

There, in the darkness of space, sat an unformed earth, void of all purpose and meaning. Covered in water and engulfed in obscurity, the spirit of God hovered over the waters. Then God spoke purpose and beauty into the formless, void planet. Light was allowed to shine as the earth began to spin round and round. Where ever the light shone,

---

[11] I do not here mean there is no explanation, but that the beginning is a puzzle to modern science.
[12] John 10:10

it was called day. The darkness was called night.

He formed the heavens with a word. He caused the land and the watery seas to be separated. Out of the land, life began to grow. Trees, grass, vines and bushes of all different types came out of the once formless terrain. Filled with purpose, each plant brought forth fruit and vegetables to nourish the future creation yet to be formed. Life was a sign that God had spoken.[13]

At His word, the sun, moon and stars were spread out. Each one placed purposefully to guide, lighten and structure life. Every created thing worked in harmony with the other. The symmetry of God was taking hold in the realm He was creating.

He spoke once more, "Let the water teem with living creatures," and the waters

[13] Genesis 1

commenced to teem with animals; great sea creatures moved through the watery depths. "Let birds fly above the earth." [14] Birds took flight and moved effortlessly on the sea breeze and over the land.

At His command, the soil of the earth produced new life. These living creatures abounded and multiplied, filling the land with flesh-and-bone life. At the close of every creative act, God said "it was good."

The very goodness of God was being expressed in His work of creation. Every word spoken, every land and sea formed and every life that abounded spoke of His greatness and goodness. It was the expression of His might and power. When the God of the universe wanted to reveal His magnificence, He made our world, the sun, moon, stars, filling the expanse of space with His power.

---

[14] Genesis 1:20

The creation of God had become like a temple, a home for God in which He could rule and reign sovereignly over all He had made.[15] There was no doubt that it was good. He made it just the way He wanted, revealing the beauty of His person in every blade of grass, every tree, and every creature on land and in sea. It was good and out of the waters of chaos God brought life and order, the type of life salvation promises.

There was still one last good creation yet to be formed. It was to be His best exhibit of power and majesty: made in His very image and after His very likeness. God made man. From the dust of the ground that had been once separated from the waters, God formed man. Once formed, He breathed into his nostrils the breath of life. Lifeless man became a living being. Now, with the pinnacle of His

---

[15] See John Walton's work, "The Lost World of Genesis One"

work complete, God looked over all He had created and said "it was very good." And there, from His heavenly throne, God rested in the house He built.

He had put man in charge, to rule and serve over all the earth, being His image in the land. The breath-filled creation of God, in all the splendor he had been given, was also given a choice. All other creatures operated innately on divine instinct. Man, however, was allowed to choose. He could choose God's way, or he could choose another path. Sadly, he chose his own course.

At that moment, all of creation changed. The very ability to create life, "be fruitful and multiply", when man was most like their God and creator, was made difficult and dangerous. The pain of birth was multiplied. What was once pure joy was now mixed with pain, and often sorrow.

The ground became cursed, hardened and difficult to cultivate. It would no longer easily produce all that was needed to give life. Man would now have to struggle to make the ground do what it was created to do. The pleasure of sowing and reaping was supplanted with the difficult and laborious task of working under the hot sun in a world where the very soil seemed to be against him.

Even the plants were cursed. Thorns and thistles grew from the ground. Harvesting the grains became tiring and toilsome. Only after much work, toil and labor, sweat and blood could they at long last try to enjoy a meal. Sweating and tired, man would eat.

The worst curse of all is that the dust man was formed from would be the grave he would be buried in. Innocence had been lost and human death had entered the world through Adam. Because of his sin, all of creation was now less than it should be. Like a shattered mirror that gives occasional glimpses of reality, the whole of the universe sits, not truly being all that it was created to be. Similarly, the very image of God in man also finds itself broken and shattered. Man is not as he should be. Man is not as God had intended him: holy and serving God's good creation. Sin seemed to be undoing the goodness He had created. Would salvation come?

The goodness of creation had been placed by God on a knifes edge. The slightest folly of man would cause it to go off balance and fall over the edge. The folly of the flesh happened, and over the side creation went. What is God to do about this; can this be fixed?

There are many who would claim that the answer, in short, is "no." They say that the once good creation of God is lost over the edge forever. All of creation has been incurably cursed. Sin lives in the hearts of men. Evil actions, addictions and hatred continually fuel mankind. God will save our souls, but not our bodies or our world. No, creation is sadly on its way to the cosmic landfill, never to be heard of or seen again.

However, this couldn't be further from the truth. God does not change. His plans for a good creation, with man reigning, ruling and serving remain faithfully intact. Even at earth's darkest moment, when the wickedness of man was at its peak in the days of Noah, God did not entirely destroy all. Instead, He made a way back; a way back to the beginning. His command to Noah and his family as they left the ark in Genesis 9:1 is the same as the instruction He gave to mankind in the beginning: "Be fruitful and multiply, and fill the earth."

Isaiah 65 speaks of a future time when God creates new heavens and a new earth. Weeping and pain shall be no more. Sorrow and death will vanish like a wicked storm falls out of sight over the eastern horizon. There will be peace, purpose and joy in the new world. His creation is good, worth redeeming. Our future hope is that one day, when the sons of God are revealed, the great new creation will take place. He will make all things new. This is the world that Isaiah invites us to imagine: a place where the afflicted shall eat and be satisfied.[16]   New creation is the promise of salvation.

This was the hope of Israel, firmly founded on the word and nature of God. In Romans 8:18-20, Paul tells us that faithful man is being re-formed into the image of His Son. In Christ, the shattered image of God is being renewed. Paul says that our hearts groan for this renewal, longing to be made whole and that our groanings are not in vain. We long to

---

[16] Psalm 22:26 (sounds similar to the sermon on the mount: Blessed are the hungry, for they shall be fed)

get back to the way we were intended to be. We long to be saved.

Paul tells us we are not alone in this groaning. All of creation joins us in the painful chorus. Together we groan and long for the same thing. The heavens, mountains, valleys, rivers and oceans groan side-by-side with us. They, too, long to be made right. They long to have the curse of the sin of man lifted. Creation was an innocent bystander in the rebellion of man. It does not groan to be destroyed, but rather to be redeemed. It longs to be delivered from the bondage of corruption. According to God's word and, indeed, His very nature, it will be made right.

We long to see the true glory that creation once was. Our inner-most being desires to experience the deep richness of a life where we can walk through un-cursed fields, swim in clean, fresh waters and walk with the Lord, the one whom we call "our God."

91

The future promise is bright and glorious. We eagerly await this new place, this new earth, with excitement and baited-breath. There is a purged and purified land where "righteousness dwells" according to 2 Peter 3:13. There is a time coming when God will make all things new. He will wipe every tear from our eyes and remove every groaning from our bodies. Death and sorrow will be no more. These are part of the old creation, the fallen creation. In the new world, they will pass away with no hope of return. These words are faithful and true.[17]

The first creation had its start with the Spirit of God hovering over the waters. Out of the water, by the power and word of God, creation came to be. When it was time to start afresh, God sent water to flood the earth. Now, when it is time to start new creation, it too begins in waters of new creation.

---

[17] Revelation 21:5

Paul tells us that the beauty of the first creation and the majesty of the creation yet to come can be experienced in our current lives. While we long for the day to arrive, when God will right all wrongs, we have the chance to bring a part of the new creation from the future into the present. We can be the image of the new world, shining in the old one.

The imagery of new creation that is spoken of in Revelation 21:5 is also seen in 2 Corinthians 5:17. Revelation speaks of a time when the old world will be done away with, along with its sorrow and death. The old is gone; the new has come. Paul says that we can be the long awaited new creation right now. The way that life will be is the way we are when we are in Christ.

The phrasing between these two passages of scripture is amazingly similar. The note to the Corinthians tells us that in Him, we are "new creation."[18]

For Paul, there is never any doubt that we find ourselves connecting with the Christ in baptism. This is where we meet Him in His death and find new life in His resurrection. Indeed, the resurrected life we live now is a foretaste of the new creation life yet to be fully realized. This is when we are clothed with the robes of the Messiah. This is where our hearts are circumcised and our sins are washed away in His flood. Here, in the water, is where we put on Jesus.

Just as the earth sat in darkness, immersed in water, with no purpose, so we too find that our lives outside of the Messiah lack lasting meaning. We know deep within us that there must be significance. There has to be a purpose that runs deeper than the daily activities of our lives.

---

[18] The article, "a" (as many translations have it) is not in the original language. Nor does the word "creature" show up. It literally says "new creation."

In the futile life of old creation, our souls desire relief. We want the darkness that engulfs us to dissipate. We want to feel the rays of the sun warm our bodies. We want to see the light of life course through our veins. The shattered image longs to be restored.

In baptism, the darkness of our old world melts away. God speaks to us on that watery road and does His marvelous work in our lives. His light shines on us, in us and through us. We show the signs of new life as His power transforms us. Out of the waters of chaos and mayhem we rise to new life. We are the new creation. We are a sign to the old world that there is a new, better world on the way. It has already started in us and one day will be completed universally.

As you stand and look at the edge of this watery road, you finally realize that there isn't a fork in the road at all. Instead, there is just one road, broad and expansive, lying before

95

you.   On all sides of the path, you see something so marvelous, so beautiful and so amazing, that you can't help but move forward. You long to be made in to the true you. You long to have the very image of God renewed in you. In baptism, the waters of new creation wash over you and bring order out of chaos. New creation has begun in you.

Wading into the Text

In what ways can you look around you and see that a new creation is desperately needed?

When you look within your own life, do you see the signs of chaos and meaninglessness, or do you see the signs of the very life of God springing out?

What part of your life needs to be left in the water so you can live as part of the new world?

New creation looks like: love, joy, forgiveness, life, relationship, reconciliation and purity. How might knowing that you are now already part of this new creation guide your life?

97

Conclusion

You no longer want to stand on the edge of this watery, baptism road. The sheer beauty and power speaks to the deepest part of your heart. In excitement, you wade into the water that lies before you. You are ankle deep in crisp, clean waters. Every step you take you find yourself moving deeper. You sense that God is doing something amazing and you must go in even further.

In over your head, you are tossed about. The waters of creation are making you a part of the new world and a new man. The Red Sea is giving you safe passage to the land of freedom, crushing and killing the Egyptian warriors that desire to drag you back to slavery. The great flood is crashing against your heart, washing away the sin that has so long governed your life. It penetrates deep, removing the sinful flesh that has grown over your heart like a callous. It offers you the robes of freedom: free from the exile and ready to serve your God and father.

As you continue to move forward, you find that you are showing signs of resurrection life. Everything is different now that you have walked the path. You are different and are called to never be the same again.

One of the most striking things about baptism is that every time it is mentioned, a different portrayal is used to describe it. It is too beautiful to be explained in one simple way. It is too powerful to be contained in a formula. In order to truly understand it, you must see it from all the various angles the scripture provides. It is the waters of new creation. It is the Red Sea that leads to freedom. It is the flood that washes us clean. It is the force that penetrates our being and cuts away the sinful flesh. It is our way to new life, new family, new man and new robes.

Baptism is the working of God's power, not man's power. It isn't just a step in a man-made process, nor is it optional and rather pointless. No, it is so much more than that. It is time for the church and every believer to reclaim the beauty, power and place of baptism. It is time to jump in and bask in the watery road to God. Amen.

Made in United States
North Haven, CT
16 March 2022

17207904R00057